THE QUEST FOR HAPPINESS

Paula Price

Book cover-SelfPubBookCovers.com/ RLSather

ISBN 979-8-9904328-0-2 (paperback)
ISBN 979-8-9904328-1-9 (Ebook)
ISBN 979-8-9904328-2-6 (hardcover)

Published by Anchor Heart
www.AnchorHeartBooks.com

This book is dedicated to all who are in the pursuit of happiness. Whether you have been on this quest for a while or are just waking up to the journey, my hat is off to you for being brave, eager to be a student of life, and being a loving human.

To the people, places, films, books, and others that helped me find my truth and light I am grateful. (Some I mention in this book.) Grateful I can pay it forward, and hope my readers can too.

Also, a special thanks to all who make up my circle and people. To those here from the past, present, and future, I thank you for being a part of my journey.

Contents

Introduction

If you were to ask me earlier this year, or any other time of my life, if I would write a book about happiness I would never have thought so. But at this time in our lives I feel like there's so much crazy and warped energy around us that we need to be wise and figure out ways we can create our own happiness no matter the circumstances. No one is going to do that for us. It is our responsibility to create every feeling that we feel. No one can make us feel a certain way, rather it is up to us to choose to feel that way within the circumstances presented. I challenge you to choose happiness even when your current situation may not normally dictate it. Remember, it is your choice and it is your life.

I am not a psychiatrist, psychologist, or someone who went to school to learn how to be happy. This is just my interpretation of life and things that I've gone through, learned along the way, and/or watched others go through. Just like I mention in this book, sit with these thoughts, and if they resonate with you, great. If they don't then don't take them to heart. It's always your choice. You are the master of your domain. I am just here to remind you of that.

I'm hoping that by reading this book you get a glimpse into things that you can do to create your own happiness. It's definitely not something that we are used to having happen all the time especially through bad times, but I think this is our salvation. I feel like this is how we escape the matrix and the crazy of our current world. If we don't let the crazy in and we focus on our own happiness, we become exactly who we were meant to be. Let this be a sounding board to create things that you discover make you happy; share them with your friends, family, and everyone you know.

   By the time you're done reading this book, you will probably know more than me about happiness. Certainly your own happiness. If I can help just one person achieve and choose happiness, I feel like I have accomplished something with this book. Here's to an enlightened journey towards happiness for you and the world.

We embark on a journey
each day of our lives.

Our choices are many
do we take them in stride?

Is it happy, or sad,
or perhaps in between?

Let's look at the prospects
and balance the unseen.

Chapter One:

Things Happen

What if everything happens for a reason? What if everything that we encounter are things that will help us get to the next place or phase in life, even the good, bad, and ugly? If we know that, then we will embrace it, grieve, let go, and move on. For example, if someone loses everything in a fire they have the choice to either become angry and bitter and go down that path of "woe is me" or the choice to decide "this was a way of making me rebuild a better life." Make no mistake, you cannot skip the steps of grieving and letting go. Most people tend to get caught up and have a hard time getting past the grieving stage to let go of it and move on to something that will actually create happiness. Yes, you are allowed to be happy. And yes it might be difficult, but the choice is happiness or not happiness. There really is no in between. People make themselves miserable because they cannot let go of something that upset them and that becomes the sounding board for everything they choose. Or it is the feeling of guilt that they cannot be happy because of what happened. If one can choose something beyond that, if one can actually see beyond that grief, vendetta, anger, or guilt;

they can then use the experience to see a better path forward. This bears repeating. You deserve to be happy!

Everything that happens comes with a choice to invest in your future. Which kind of investment do you want to make? What if everyone in your life is just playing a part and they aren't assigned to either being good or bad; rather, it's just things that happen to help you achieve what you came into this life to achieve; whatever it is that you were supposed to do in this lifetime. Therefore, you can't look at people or things as bad or good, but as ways to help you heal and get to the next level or place that you're supposed to be. If someone does something to upset you or anger you, maybe it's to make you see things a different way or to look into yourself to ask why it angers you. Maybe it's time that that person is no longer in your life.

There are a myriad of reasons why people act the way they do and most, if not all of them, have nothing to do with you. You just have to figure out if it's someone that you see moving you forward, is neutral, or takes you down a path you would rather not venture. And it's OK because like I said before, everyone is here to play their part. Perhaps we really did make a contract with each other before coming into this life to learn lessons. Either way, life is short and we are responsible for our own choices and actions regardless of what others do to us. It bears repeating – we need to grieve, let go, and then choose happiness.

Ultimately, everything in our life is a choice and, especially with the older generations, we were so conditioned to the programming that we received from the media and in schools, that we think things are exactly what we were told. We think, "that's just the way it is", and don't really put a lot more thought into it. I want to teach the new generations to think for themselves and to do things that school didn't teach us, like meditation and connection to the higher self. I want people to know that they actually have a choice in life. That they can actually change their mindset and change their world. We all make a difference. We are all important.

We need to stop blaming others for our circumstances for our place in life. We can only choose for ourselves how we want things to be for us. I know this is not a normal thought process because again, people tend to blame other people and circumstances for where they are in life instead of taking responsibility. We are even taught this is the case. It's almost like school and media teach us that it is OK to think, "I am here because of my environment and circumstances". Schools are not exactly teaching that statement, it is merely a mindset and that you can overcome circumstances simply by knowing that you can overcome them. If we don't give people the perception that it is possible for them to overcome things, they never will. Look at the people that blame their circumstances for where they are in life. These people will never achieve success or happiness because they are going to continually blame the system, or where they grew up, their parents, or anyone around them for the problems with their life. Then, there are others who were able to come out of that negative space and gain much success because they never let that hold them back. What makes them "defy the odds"? Their mindset!

Look at what the world has shown us about war throughout history. We always say things like, "Oh they are the evil ones!", " It's their fault!", "They deserve it because they did something to us first.", etc. but there will be no peace and no happiness until we let go of those thoughts and realize everything that enters into our life view is a choice that we are making consciously. Two wrongs do not make a right. And no war or conflict will solve anything with the mindset of war and conflict. It is only when we realize that we are all humans working together that we can collectively achieve peace, love, and happiness. But I think the key is that it is always our own choice. And this is a huge awakening.

A wonderful example of this choice is the film *Life is Beautiful*. The film tells the story of a father and son who are forced into a concentration camp during World War II. In the film, the father uses his imagination to make their life seem beautiful for his son even though they are living through horrific circumstances. You can have the shittiest of circumstances and still choose to rise above them and make something out of nothing. Life is short so what are you waiting for?

When something happens that makes you sad or angry or completely lost, allow yourself to feel. You cannot bury an emotion and expect to be able to be completely happy. Sometimes this could take a very long time but this does not mean you cannot have moments of happiness and choose to do things that will give you moments of pure joy even when going through the toughest of times. Make a list of things that make you happy. When you are feeling depressed you need to find a way out of it and sometimes it's just action that can get you out of the mood. Everything around us is energy so changing your environment and energy can create all the difference in how we feel. Are you inside your house? Then go outside and walk around in the grass, feeling the Earth beneath your feet. Are you outside? Go inside and make yourself a hot cup of tea and listen to your favorite songs. Whatever you are doing, change the space you are in and you will notice a difference in energy and feeling.

Time for some fun. Make a list of at least three things in your life that have prevented you from moving forward. It could be someone that made you angry or something that you feel like you are not good enough or a life circumstance that you feel is keeping you down. If you can't think of anything right now just come back to it when you do.

1._____
_____

2_____
_____

3._____
_____

Some days you have to actively create happiness. Sometimes you have to fake it till you make it. You are a reflection of your outer world. Pretending that you're happy can also spark real happiness. If you feel love, then you will experience it. The idea is to turn inward, not outward. You must feel love from the inside, not the outer world. Are you actively doing things that make you happy?

Make a list of three things that you can do that will immediately change your space and environment to create happiness. Allow yourself to write things down as they come to you and do not overthink what comes up. You might be surprised at what you can discover. In the next chapters, I will give you many ideas if you cannot think of any on your own. You can come back and write them later. Come back here to remind yourself. Add and change up your favorites as much as you need to.

1._____

_____

2._____

_____

3._____

_____

Things happen for a reason that
we may not know at the time.

Perhaps they bring us to places
we otherwise would never find.

Know we can over come things
and be better in the end.

Life is a wonderful journey
when we let it be our friend.

Chapter Two:

Nuts and Bolts

What is happiness? The Webster's Dictionary defines it as, "a state of wellbeing and contentment". That is not very informative or explanatory. That definition can be vague unless you know what contentment feels like. Do we really know what happiness or contentment feel like? Is it the same for everyone? The answer is probably no. For this books purpose, I want you to think of happiness as the feeling of joy and the feeling that you don't want this very moment to end because you are enjoying it so much. Have you ever felt that? What moment can you think of that brought you those feelings?

Love and happiness go hand-in-hand. Do you know what love feels like? What if we were able to walk into a closet and get recharged and feel the love energy all around us whenever we wanted. Unfortunately, I'm not sure they've come up with that technology quite yet but it would be really cool if they did. We can, however, create a space and place that makes us happy and want to project our own love. This is something that we can definitely do, we just have to create it for ourselves. Most of the time humans expect to get love from outside sources and when they don't get it, they feel disappointed and rejected. Love needs to come from within first, from your own heart and soul. The more you give it to other people, the more you will feel it in return. If you look for it outside of yourself, you will usually be just disappointed. And when others hurt us we take it personally.

I would say 98% of the time when someone hurts you, it doesn't have anything to do with you. It is their own jealousy, self sabotage, or other issues that make them do the things they do. This is a really big concept because if you realize that other people's behavior has nothing to do with you, you can stop taking it personally. I fully believe that the people who bully or do bad things to people simply need more love. Perhaps these people actually need more love because they don't know what love feels like and they are missing it from their life. Most people have not learned the art of self love. A well known family therapist, Virginia Satir said, "We need 4 hugs a day for survival. We need 8 hugs a day for maintenance. We need 12 hugs a day for growth." I'm not sure if this is true, but it would definitely be great to start giving out hugs each day. The more love you expand outward, the more you feel inward, and the happier you are within yourself.

So how do we practice self-love? There are obviously many ways, but a simple way to start is to practice proper hygiene and nutrition. If you don't take care of your body, or you are feeling sluggish because you were putting junk food into it, how can you expect to sustain true happiness? Everything that comes into our body is a reflection of what we are, and what we become. I don't think anyone wants to become a big disheveled, greasy piece of fried fat. Can you truly be happy without proper nutrition and care for your body? Your body simply will not be able to support you. It might be obvious, but if you wake up feeling down, getting up to brush your teeth, wash your face, or do some morning stretches can be a good start to feeling better. Eating a healthy meal to put some positive fuel into your body is also helpful. Interestingly, studies have shown that the mere act of smiling releases endorphins that make us feel better and lift our mood. So make sure to smile as often as you need to.

If you aren't feeling healthy, you will have a harder time becoming happy. It seems pretty obvious, but when you are sick, you need to rest and take care of yourself. Having a good regiment will also help your immune system. Know that it is absolutely OK to rest. Even if you aren't sick, some times we just need a day off. Never make yourself feel guilty for needing that. You deserve it. You work hard at life every day and when you feel like you need some rest, take it.

A few other things to remember about healthy habits and happiness are that diet, exercise, and getting enough sleep, affect you. If you're eating something with low energy, you're putting that into your body and are going to give yourself low energy. Things that won't help in the long run are drugs and alcohol. Drinking to forget will only work until you remember again, so work on your traumas to heal them instead. (We will talk about this in more depth in the following chapters.) If you find you are consuming an excess of alcohol or junk foods, there might be underlying reasons for that, or perhaps you just love the taste. Either way, try and cut down on bad foods and add whole foods back into your diet so that your body has better fuel to burn.

Having an exercise plan in place is also a must for consistent positive energy flow. qigong, yoga, Pilates, even walking daily or hiking are great energy flow workouts. There are many other possibilities for exercise depending on your health, age, and needs; but whether it's chair exercises or full out cardio, having a daily time for exercise will help your energy flow. It will also help to alleviate stress. Figure out a good time for you to exercise daily so that it prepares you for good sleep. Some people find exercising before work, school, or at the start of their day energizes them. Others find that exercise later in the day helps them wind down and release the day's tension. Whichever works for you is what you should implement into your schedule, but remember to get enough sleep so you aren't burning the candle at both ends. Without proper sleep, your body can't be expected to function enough to bring about happiness.

What are some self-love skills you could master better? (Getting more sleep, setting up an exercise plan, and cutting out just a day's worth of junk food are a few ideas.)

1._____

2._____

3._____

A good fact to keep in mind is that every body type is different. You need to love your body, whether it is heavy, thin, curvy, or round because it is part of who you are. There is no body that is truly perfect living on this earth. You definitely need to love yourself completely no matter what to be happy. You may decide you want to lose a few pounds or color your gray hairs, but the essence of yourself, your inner core and soul is what is important. The essence of you is what you need to love and embrace, not your outward appearance. A person who loves themself, and therefore their body, will continue to better themselves by feeding their body and giving it the best care they can. That doesn't mean you will have a perfect figure, weight, or frame. Do the best you can and your body will appreciate you. Just like money can't buy happiness, even if you were the prettiest or handsomest person in the room, if you don't love the inner core being of yourself, you will not be happy.

Doing things that make you happy is a must when it comes to self-love. Do you know what makes you happy? Don't wait for someone or something to save you. Waiting around for your prince or princess to come will not make you happy. You need to be your own prince or princess. As was mentioned before, you need to be the creator of your own love for yourself and generate your own happiness. No one else is responsible for that but you. And the crazy thing is, until you truly love yourself, you won't be able to sustain a healthy relationship because you need to love yourself first.

So many times when we feel anger or frustration, we reach out to the first person we see to share our anger or frustration and just keep the frustration going. Now you have also spread the energy of frustration to your friend or family member and it will affect them. It is much more productive to take that frustration and channel it into something productive. If something angers you, write about it, draw or paint a picture about it, go outside and plant some seeds, etc. Allow that energy to manifest in a different way. In the next few chapters, I will give you several ideas on things you can do to create your own happiness. You will be able to change your energy and lighten the space around you

An important point to remember is that if we don't see or feel our emotions, we can't transcend them. So yes, make sure you are true to yourself and acknowledge everything you're feeling. Letting go is not to regret the past, but to grow and live for the future. You can also channel that into creative outlets and create happiness even in the midst of crisis. This is really the only reason we are here. It's simple. We are here for such a short time that if you don't take advantage of every moment you have, you are simply not taking advantage of every moment you have.

Just to reiterate, you must acknowledge your emotions, but don't let them engulf your entire existence. Here's a good exercise. What are some of the core beliefs you have about yourself? What are you telling yourself that might not be kind? Sit with these questions and notice what you tell yourself throughout your day. If you notice you are being hard on yourself, ask yourself why. We tend to call ourselves stupid, fat, ugly, or many other upsetting things. Start becoming aware of things you tell yourself and try to make them positive. Remember, each day you are doing your best to finding happiness.

Write down a few things you told yourself that are negative.

1._____

2._____

3._____

Now turn those things around and write them as a positive. So if you are telling yourself you are stupid, write it out as, "I am learning to be smarter everyday by learning from my mistakes."

1._____

_____

2._____

_____

3._____

_____

When we start speaking to ourselves more positively, we will begin to learn to love ourselves more and simultaneously become happier. Happiness is a journey that continues daily. As new events happen in our lives they can try to tire us, demotivate us, and even bring us pain. Try to be aware when this happens so that you can shift your thoughts from negative feelings to feelings where you can use them to evolve and become more accepting of the journey and where it can take you. Sometimes bad things happen so that we can learn from them. Decide that they are a gift. Discover strategies for resilience and self discovery in the face of life's challenges. Adopt a mindset for growth and choose positivity in the midst of adversity.

In the next two chapters, I will share a few ideas on what you can do and use to shift your perspective and your energy to be more positive and happy each day

What is happiness we want to know.

Is it fixed or does it come and go?

If we listen to our heart and mind,

eternal happiness we will surely find.

Chapter Three:

Nature Doesn't Have an Agenda

Probably one of the best places to go or thing to do to find happiness is to get outside in nature. Nature does not have an agenda, nor will it try to make you do things or say things that you don't want to. It is just there for the giving and taking. If you live by the mountains, take a hike in them. If you live by the beach, sit and watch the ocean. Sometimes, just going for a walk can change your mood. Basically, whatever you are in the middle of doing, change it up. Even if you live in an apartment, you can sit outside on your balcony or open the window and breathe in the fresh air. Nature is always there just doing it's thing. It has no ego. We can be reminded of the present moment's gift by admiring it.

Have you heard of grounding? Another term for it is earthing. Call it either, but it can be a wonderful healing experience and bring about happiness. For this purpose, the easiest way to try it out and practice grounding is to take your shoes off and walk in grass or dirt or even lie down in grass or dirt and feel the energy coming from it. Just breathe in and out and stay as long as you need to get connected to the earth. Feel the earth's energy and feel connected to something larger than yourself.

There are so many things you can do in nature to feel connected and happy. Here are a few thoughts and I have added space at the end for you to add your own to the list.

1. Similar to grounding, you can get in water to swim or exercise or even just hang out in it. This will also help you feel connected to something bigger. Of course, you must practice water safety.

2. Sit on the beach and watch the sunrise or sunset. The beach can be a very peaceful place to spend your time. You don't even have to be there during the sunrise or sunset to listen to the waves. I like to go find a spot without a lot of people. However, you might find the noise of other people laughing and playing help with the sense of happiness for you. If you don't want to sit, you can also comb the beach for shells or walk along the water and feel the sand beneath your toes. If you do find any shells, you can take them and keep them as a token for when you can't get to the beach. (Unless of course that beach has rules against that)

3. Plant a garden. This can actually be a bigger project as you can return to this daily and even make a special place in it to meditate etc. Be it a vegetable or a flower garden, the choice is yours. You could even choose to do both. If you don't live in a climate

that allows this year-round, consider bringing some nature indoors and planting a small herb garden or flowers inside in a special area in your house or apartment. You could also start vegetables inside before replanting them outside when it gets warmer.

4. If you can't plant a garden, most communities have community gardens where you can help out, or find your local flower or vegetable farm. They usually have picking times for different vegetables or flowers that are in season. Take your time to roam the grounds and again don't forget to take in all of the small things you see. How does the sun hit the plants? What insects are climbing on the plants? What animals can you hear in the distance? When we stop and take time to notice our surroundings it helps ground us in the present and we don't dwell on the past and things we can't control.

5. Sit outside and watch the local animals. We started feeding the squirrels during the pandemic and they still come around a few years later. We actually named them all because they each have different personalities. You don't have to watch or feed squirrels. There might be birds, rabbits, deer and possibly many other animals in your neighborhood and community. It can be fun to take note of all of them and see how often they come around and what their habits are.

6. Adopt or foster a pet. Yes this is not something to take lightly but there are so many animals out

there that need a good home and if you want to feel unconditional love and happiness it might be something to consider. Especially if you live alone, it can be a great asset to know that someone is always there with you. If you don't feel you could actually take on the responsibility of caring for a pet 24/seven, why not "adopt one for the day". I'm sure there are many friends out there who would let you borrow theirs for the day, or better yet, go visit a shelter and volunteer or visit them for the day. They could use the mutual love.

7. Be active in nature. Being in nature doesn't have to mean walking in a forest or being in the middle of a pasture. It simply means you are getting outside. Go for a hike, a walk, or a bike ride. Action creates new energy. When you are actively moving it can regenerate your soul. Endorphins will also kick in, helping you to feel better. Make sure you take the time to enjoy your surroundings. Look for the little things. Watch a butterfly in-flight or the tiniest bug climb on a tree. This will help you be present in the moment.

8. Find or take photos of your favorite places you have visited in nature. Keep a photo album of these pictures on your phone, device, or print them out and put them in a physical album. These are things you can look at to spark memories and happiness.

9. Similarly, you can search for videos of your favorite places or locations that you would like to

travel to. You can even take some time to envision a dream vacation and start manifesting getting there. Every day when you watch the videos, it's almost like you are there. You can also create a folder to store ideas of places that you would like to travel to and/or make a bucket list.

10. Eat outside. Take your coffee or breakfast outside and sit in your backyard or balcony (open a window if you live in an apartment without a balcony). Listen to the animals and plants. Take in the way everything around you makes you feel. It's a great way to start your day and tune in to nature knowing that the day will be amazing. You can also take your lunch or dinner to a near by park if you are stuck in an office all day. Change up your scenery.

11. There are other ways to enjoy nature and help it at the same time. You can join a conservation group or do your own litter walk where you pick up trash around your area, the beach, park, etc. It always feels good helping out so it's a win win. You could even start a new hobby such as Upcycling, where you can create art out of water bottles or other waste materials you find. Just make sure to wash everything and keep everything clean. You could even play a game of geocaching while you're at it.

These are just a few ideas of things that can get you out into nature and create a new vibration of happiness for you. Use these as a guide but know there are so many more things you can do. Gaia, Mother Earth, is always there showing us harmony and unity through nature.

It's especially important if you work indoors all day to get outside when you aren't working. You can even get some vitamin D if you time it right with the sun. Scientifically, sunlight has many benefits including improving sleep (it can reset our circadian rhythm), reducing stress, fighting off depression, and strengthening the immune system.

Here is some space to write a few of your own ideas. (What are things you like to do or want to try in nature?)

1._____

_____

2._____

_____

3._____

_____

4._____

_____

5._____

_____

The beauty of nature cannot be untold.

Its brilliance and vigor is a sight to behold.

When we need to be lifted and filled with great light.

It's nature's pure allure that will set us toward right.

Chapter Four:

Tried and True or Something New

What makes someone happy? Is it a pure quest each day to be happy? Is it a drive? Is it will power? Sometimes it's the comfort of something we did previously with a family or a friend that brings us great memories or sometimes it's the joy of simply trying something new that we've always wanted to. Either way, happiness can be found in these simple day to day activities.

Why am I talking about everyday activities and sharing some ideas of what you can do? Sometimes, we just need to get out of our head and do something that brings us joy. Yes, I'm sure you already know all of these things, but it is a reminder that actively making choices to do fun things is something that should always be on your to-do list. Big or small, it doesn't matter. Find joy in the smallest of activities.

Make sure to always make time for fun. Life just isn't about punching time cards and making money. Make time for things you love to do too. Here are some thoughts for fun things that hopefully will spark some new or tried and true ideas for you.

1. Take a cooking class. You can even try a different sort of style or cultural food. Many stores that sell kitchen items have classes, your parks and recreation system may sometimes offer classes, or even a culinary school might have some open classes.

2. Take an exercise class. Try something new. If you are used to doing yoga, try aerobics. If you are used to high impact exercise try Pilates or qigong. Switch it up between endurance, strength, balance, and flexibility. Movement and exercise also allows stuck energy to flow so you can heal and feel happier. Even if you can't afford to join a gym or pay for a consistent class there are hundreds of free workouts on the internet you can look up and try.

3. Learn a new hobby like knitting or bowling. Think of something you have always wanted to try but perhaps you were too scared, or didn't want to do it by yourself. You might start off by yourself but you'll probably make a new friend by doing something new. You could also ask a friend to take you to one of their classes as a guest or swap hobbies with them. You can teach them how to cook the lasagna you make that they love, and in exchange, they can teach you how to play golf.

4. Visit a friend. Maybe you aren't the only one who needs positive energy. Bring lunch to a friend, ask a friend to a movie, or call an old friend you haven't talked to in a while. As we get older, we tend to get so wrapped up in our day to day to do list, that we forget to make time for fun or connection with friends. Set aside time each week to rekindle and nurture your connections.

5. Volunteer with children or senior citizens. Helping others allows you to take your focus off of yourself which can sometimes help you realize you're better off than you think you are. When you give love, you get love. Some places you could volunteer at include local senior centers, charity organizations, or homeless shelters.

6. Find a space that will help you grow spiritually. Whether that's a church, mosque, synagogue, Buddhist temple, or healing center, it doesn't matter. You could even sit out in nature and create your own spiritual space. Another fun thing to try when it comes to religion is to go visit another religion that is not yours. When you see what others believe and put your feet in their shoes it can be very eye-opening and enlightening. You don't need religion to have spiritual growth but you might find one that helps your journey.

7. Host a game night with your friends or family. Sometimes just getting out and being around other people to do something fun lightens the mood.

Similarly, you could host a movie night, a potluck, or anything that surrounds you with people you know and love. Don't have the space to host it? Enlist a friend to cohost that does, or have it at a community center.

8. Go to a spa, get a pedicure, or anything that will help with your self-care. Even the manliest of men enjoy a good spa day. If the spa is too expensive, set the mood at home. Run a bath, paint your toes, and sip your favorite relaxing beverage. Go ahead and pamper yourself.

9. Bake some goodies and/or write an encouraging note to a neighbor and secretly drop it off on their front porch or in their mailbox. When we do things for others, it takes our focus off of our self and any of the day's problems. You will feel like you have accomplished something and that will bring about happiness. It's also just satisfying to see someone else smile.

As in the last chapter, these are just a few ideas that hopefully will spark some of your own ideas about things that you can do that make yourself happy. What others can you think of? Don't get too caught up in having it be something really extravagant. It can be something as simple as reading a romance novel or as new as taking a class in marketing. It could be something you never make time to do anymore or something you have never done before.

You can write a few of your own here.

1._____

2._____

3._____

What we do daily can create a great life.

If we strive to enjoy each day and each night.

Our choices can take us to places unknown.

Happiness comes from the affections we have grown.

Chapter Five:

Meditation and Healing

Remember who you truly are. The forces around you want you to forget. You are a beautiful human full of the capability to love and be loved. Before you can truly resonate love, you must heal your trauma. We have lots of trauma, from the collective trauma from thousands of years of our civilization, to things we've experienced in this lifetime. Trauma is anything that has caused you to have anxiety or mental distress, and it can stem from something straightforward like someone bullying you as a child, or being caught in a storm to something deeper like rape or abuse. Open your body and mind to happiness and pay attention to what you focus on and the emotion or meaning that you give to what you focus on.

Take time each day for meditation (self reflection/ prayer) and to heal whatever traumas or experiences you may be holding onto in your body. It's important to tune out the noise. (The noise that others create and also noise you create to stop listening to yourself.) You can start your day with it and/or end your day with this practice. If you have never meditated before, here is a simple "how to" below to help you get started. There are many videos on the internet that you can find and watch if you would like to get a little bit more advanced or creative. If you resonate more with prayer or self reflection you can also do that. Anything that gets you out of your own way is key.

Find a comfortable place to sit with no outside distractions. You can play soft relaxing music in the background if you would like. Close your eyes. Start with your toes and mentally work your way all the way up to your head making sure each muscle and joint in your body is relaxed. Picture yourself sitting in a safe space –either somewhere you have been before that you felt completely happy and relaxed or a space completely made up in your mind that you know you will feel safe in. Take a deep breath in through your nose and out through your mouth. Continue to do so until you feel completely relaxed and you have all of your day's thoughts out of your mind. Tell yourself you want to be happy today, release your trauma, and set an intention. Continue to sit in this space for as long as you need to. End the meditation thanking the universe or higher power for the opportunity for another day.

If you continue your meditation practice daily, you could feel a lot different about your life in less than a week. Of course it may take you a bit longer, or maybe you aren't feeling able to make it work for you yet. Just keep trying if the latter is the case. Learn to listen to yourself and your higher consciousness. What are you telling yourself? What are you feeling and thinking? Remember that what you focus on expands so if you are holding onto negative thoughts, they will continue to grow.

One thing you can try is to experiment with sounds and frequencies for healing the chakras. The healing frequency that brings about positive transformation is 528Hz. It is said to be the ancient "solfeggio frequency" also known as the "love frequency" or the "vibration of love". You can find the perfect meditation music by searching online for it this way. If you aren't familiar with the body's chakras, they are essentially spinning discs of energy that should remain open in order to support one's emotional and physical well being. If a chakra's energy becomes blocked, it triggers an imbalance. There are seven chakra's in the body –crown, third eye, throat, heart, solar plexus, sacral, and root. There is much to learn about them, so if you are interested in learning more, I encourage you to do so. Below I will give you a basic explanation of chakras and music frequencies for meditation purposes and balance.

Here are the seven healing solfeggio frequencies for the seven chakras.

· 396Hz is for the root chakra (base of spine) and can destroy unconscious blockages, help overcome fear, and basic needs challenges.
· 417Hz is for the sacral chakra (lower abdomen) and can remove negative energy.

- 528Hz is for the solar plexus chakra (around the navel) and, as stated above, can bring positive transformation and is known as the love frequency.
- 639Hz is for the heart chakra (center of chest) and can create harmony in relationships.
- 741Hz is for the throat chakra and helps to remove toxins from the body,
- 852 Hz is for the third eye chakra (between the eyebrows) and connects to a higher power source leaving you with a greater sense of joy, peace, etc.
- 963Hz is for the crown chakra (top of head) and connects us to higher consciousness and oneness with all things.

In the beginning, I encourage you to start making a daily commitment to meditating. Once you have been doing it for a while, you can look for new ways and seek out different frequencies of music to play with. Notice anything that comes up while you are meditating and make sure you pay attention and give yourself space to heal whatever comes up.

When something happens in your life that creates unhappiness, sit with that energy. You need to deal with it and allow it to come up. Don't walk in fire. Harness the power of your emotions rather than let the emotions rush through you. This means you might actually need to take time to allow yourself to grieve and then heal. Like I said before, that doesn't mean that you can't find happiness within these moments. Knowing that this is something you need to work through should make you grateful that you realized it, and can use it as a gift to be able to work through it. Use your happy moments to allow for healing and peace. As crazy as it sounds, allow yourself to be happy that you are working through your problems and trauma. It is a gift that will help you through the other side of it and lead to a better life.

Using a real life example, imagine that a friend of yours disrespects you but they do not see it nor will they acknowledge it. You have the choice to continue that friendship or allow them to be themselves and realize the relationship no longer serves you and that you have the power to find a new friendship. Perhaps it's just what you needed to get out of your comfort zone and try something new. Maybe you will meet someone in that new cooking class you take that will lead you on the path to find a new job or meet your husband. We just never know why people come in and out of our life but acknowledging it and then allowing it to run its course and take us to new places as a result is actually a blessing. Most of us think that it's disheartening and that life is horrible when these things happen, but it's really just a way to get us to do what we should be doing.

Use meditation as a tool to think through the thoughts of the day or simply sit quietly and take in the moment. Pay attention to what you focus on and what meaning you give it or emotion you feel with it. Each moment we have the choice to move forward or stay stuck. Triggers can make us stuck or just make us feel bad (or both).

Learn to become aware of your triggers. What are the spaces, the places, and the people that create triggers for you? What are the spaces, the places, and people who make you feel uplifted? Think about your daily life. Do you get triggered when you are on your way to school or work? Does it create stress for you? Maybe it's seeing an ex lover or friend? There are so many things that can trigger us and put us into a state of anger or stress. The key is to be aware of these things so that you can heal the parts in you that become triggered. Journaling and meditating are great ways to discover these triggers and also things that can uplift you by just thinking about them.

As in the earlier meditation example, you can start with the relaxation technique and once you are relaxed, start to ask yourself who or what triggers you. What is the first thing that pops into your mind? You can journal about the meditation experience once you are finished. The more you know about what triggers you, the better decisions you can make to stay happy. Until you are healed from a triggering person or situation, you should avoid it. Allow your feelings to come through and then let them go. Once you feel good about where you are with each situation or person, you will be able to stand strong around them.

Give yourself time each day to come back to who you truly are. This might be difficult for some because it's not something you do regularly. Maybe you continue to cut yourself down. Maybe you continue to begrudge what life has dealt you. But when you sit quietly and think about the person that you truly are –your dreams, your aspirations– you can sense the good in you. You know you are good and you deserve to be happy. Take time every day to reflect on this.

Feel your feelings. I am not saying that by choosing happiness, you forget what is happening that caused you trauma, etc. I am merely stating that creating happiness needs to be a daily task for you. But at the same time, you do need to acknowledge any feelings that you have and work through them. If you aren't aware of your own trauma, you will send your anger into others.

Some things that can cause unhappiness include forgetting your true worth. Maybe you had a teacher, parent, or even a friend that told you or made you feel like you weren't good enough. Know that when others tell you these things it is merely a reflection of how they see themselves. Learn to get to know you and your gifts. No matter what you have been told in the past or may even currently be told, you have a gift to offer the world. You can be of service to others with this gift when you realize it which will in turn create happiness instead of trauma.

Another similar mental state that can cause trauma instead of happiness is comparing yourself to others. Like in the example before about not knowing your worth, comparing your worth to someone else's is simply not going to bring about happiness or enlightenment. Maybe your sibling got more attention than you. Maybe it was always your best friend that received the accolades. As stated before, everyone has their own gift. That is what makes us different. When you focus on other's wins and accomplishments instead of your own, you will always be met with disappointment. You will always be one step behind them. Learn to be happy for others as you search for your own gifts and wins. When you are truly happy for others it will open up the possibilities of your own wins and gifts instead of trying to copy and be jealous by prioritizing things that aren't really important to you in the long run. With this always comes the need for patience. Your time will come.

Worrying about the future and everything in between can also cause trauma and blocks. First of all, turn off the news. Trust me when I say that if you need to know something, you will find out about it. The news and much of the programming out there in our world today really has the sole purpose of fear mongering. If you don't believe that, watch it for a few minutes and see how you feel afterwards. Turn it off and use the time to work on yourself instead.

There are so many things that can trigger our unhappiness and a path away from one's true self and gifts (happiness). Others include not feeling like we can move out of our comfort zones. You can't try anything new if you are afraid to. What if your gift actually lies outside of your comfort zone? It's easy to get stuck where we feel safe but allow yourself to try new things and experiences. Don't get so caught up in your ego that you feel the need to be perfect at everything or always be right.

A trigger or trauma doesn't have to be associated with violence or something horrible that happened in your past. It can be something in our world collective like watching a war unfold on social media, or realizing the many atrocities we have experienced as a collective earth over the past thousands of years. Just be honest and open with yourself to be able to heal any wounds you have associated in your mind. Horrible things do happen but that is also part of our humanity at this point in our timeline. We learn that suffering can teach us lessons but we must acknowledge and move past them. Will we allow humans to suffer in the future? Are we ok with wars, famine, global dominance? That is perhaps another book but yes, these things exist and we must learn to acknowledge and share our gifts of service to the world in spite of them.

Like energy begets like energy. Surround yourself with people who make you feel loved and you can love in return. Sometimes this changes during our life as we grow and become the people we are meant to be. Learn to trust yourself and your instincts.

Think about things that trigger you. Things that make you worry or feel bad about yourself, etc. These are the things we need to heal to truly accept happiness into our lives. For example, does watching the news trigger fear? Stop watching it. At least until you can see it as something separate from yourself. Does going to a concert trigger anxiety? Try to see why. Are there too many people? Or maybe you had a bad experience at one? There are so many things that hold us back and trigger us to be unhappy. Sometimes it's even certain people that bring about a feeling. Remember that your feelings are yours and anything that doesn't feel right is something you need to look into.

List a few of your triggers here.

1._____

_____

2._____

_____

3._____

_____

What can you do to heal them?

1._____

_____

_____

2._____

_____

_____

3.-_____

_____

_____

Who or what makes you happy either by thinking of them/it, seeing them/it?

1._____

_____

_____

2._____

_____

_____

3.-_____

_____

_____

These triggers and even things that make you happy will obviously change throughout your life, so update them whenever you feel you're stressed or angry. Even when you feel loved and at peace, make a note of it. Keeping a log of these things will help you to see the overall picture.

How many times do the same triggers pop up? If they happen a lot, it is time to really examine how you are healing from them. You can also see the people or things you continue to be happy with and can feel grateful.

In stillness and silence are a healing balm,

meditation whispers a soothing psalm.

Healing our traumas and bringing in light.

Seeking a future that's limitless and bright.

Chapter Six:

Happiness School

Schools of today were created decades ago during the industrial revolution. They were around to create worker bees and people really weren't supposed to think outside the box. But that time period has ended, and we really need something new for our children. Even adults would benefit from an education built upon unity, love, and happiness. Nowadays, going to a typical college doesn't guarantee you a job like it used to. And you may just wind up with nothing but debt. Obviously, things like becoming a doctor or a lawyer require a lot more school and more generalized education, but for the average person who wants to start their own business or simply make a living doing something they love, there are so many more skills that we are not allowing the youth of today to discover. We have been trained to move away from joy and being individuals. A typical education doesn't even include important life skills. Joy is not taught in school. We are also taught that to make money, we have to go to school and not necessarily love our job. We aren't taught that if we change our thinking we can change our world.

What if we could have a school for the children of the world that would teach them things that would actually help them grow to become emotionally stable and loving adults? It is certainly not the education system that we see today. There would be no indoctrination or propaganda. They would teach meditation, relaxation tools, and skills to get through our day in a loving, compassionate way. They would teach people that love, connection, and purpose are what everyone needs and they would help people achieve those things and teach that there is a connection to heart, mind, and love. This school can be created with and through each of us.

What are some of the things that could be taught? I would love to see the true history of the planet and humanity taught along with how we are connected to the universe. Questions like why we are here and what is our purpose should be taught, because each of us has one. While we really don't know who or what else is "out there", why not teach everyone to question and research everything we can? How about teaching the connection to sensory ways of being and our soul/higher power? You don't have to teach it with religion, but there is definitely a higher power or source that keeps us all together and creates us to be who we are. If you ask a child questions on what they perceive things such as angels, higher self, etc., what would they say? At an early age, kids still remember their connection. As we get older we forget due to the environment around us. But if school taught us to embrace it, would we still remember this as adults? Until these things are taught in schools, it is up to us to seek out this knowledge for ourselves. It is our job to question the things we don't feel right about and research them.

Students should be taught how to get out of their head and into their heart. Create a connection to their expression and higher-self/higher power. If we keep that alive in children they will always be able to express themselves even as adults. Teaching love of our bodies and minds, meditation skills, and service to others as projects would be key subjects. Perhaps they would involve circle time to share and connect. Traditional teachings tell us that pain or diseases are always caused from some outside source or injury. The reality is that it's because of disease from something in our lives, with our past or present and results in the energy being stored in our body somewhere without letting it go. Let's add that in as a subject.

It is not only children that could be taught at the school. Education is for life. Adults should never stop learning how to be happy, how to truly live, and how to give and receive love. It is why we are here on earth. We should be able to experience it every day. We need to learn that the real school lies within us and truth can be found wherever we seek it from within. Most people look to outside leaders and sources for answers because we've been taught to. What if we were taught to trust our selves and our intuition?

Unfortunately we are taught from a young age that we should care about possessions and material things. These things do not sustain happiness though. Happiness does not live in bigger houses, expensive cars, or larger bank accounts. Everywhere we look, we are told we need this product or that product to be happy. We buy the products, and they do not make us happy. We really don't know why we're unhappy, so we keep buying new products and bigger things. It is not until we realize the material possessions cannot truly make us happy that we will even have the chance to be happy.

I remember watching a documentary called *Minimalism* on Netflix. The film follows people who live happier lives with fewer possessions and material things. It seems to be true that the more we want material things, the more money we will have to make, and the longer hours we will have to work. This might be fine if you love your work, but even if you truly love your work, you shouldn't spend your entire existence doing it. It should be taught that you cannot buy happiness.

Happiness is a flowing heart. It is something that you get when you can outwardly express yourself all the time. Being able to be creative and expressive is a goal that can be taught in this happiness school. Of course there will be lessons we don't always like, but if they help us to rid us of our traumas or teach us life skills, then there is much benefit towards happiness. Especially after the covid years, kids (and adults too) tend to feel a lot of anxiety and tension. What if we learned in school ways to decrease it? How about a self-help class? Self-love? Daily maintenance? Healthy diet, exercise and self-love techniques would be a great addition to any school day. Also, teaching kids life lessons like how to pay taxes, acquire financial freedom, and form their own businesses would be a fabulous addition. But that is probably another book. I'm not sure these institutions really want to keep/help us to be happy, but either way, it's all the more reason to trust in yourself to create your own happiness. Seek out ways for yourself and your family members to keep a sense of happiness in your lives.

Happiness school wouldn't just be for kids. Happiness is something we can constantly work on throughout our lives. Adults are taught that once they graduate from high school or college, education is over, but it should never end. There is so much about life that we can continue to learn especially as we get older. Knowledge is power and the more you continue to learn the more empowered you will become. Since there is no happiness school out there yet, at least not one that I know of, it's up to you to create that for yourself. Maybe one of you will start a real happiness school.

When you choose to seek out knowledge, it can open many doors for you and spark new interests and hobbies. Never give up on learning no matter your age. I find joy in learning new ideas and seeing where those ideas take me. I am definitely not the same person I was in my youth because I never stopped learning about myself and the world around me. If I pick up a new skill along the way, even better!

What are some things you want to learn about? How can learning these things help continue your happiness journey? How about a new life skill or hobby? How about learning a healing technique like Reiki or qigong? You could also learn about higher consciousness, your gifts of purpose, or astrology. Think outside the traditional box. Think about all the things you'd like to learn.

Make a list of at least 3 things you'd like to learn. Maybe you can even teach something to others?

1._____

_____

_____

2._____

_____

_____

3._____

_____

_____

We weren't really taught how to be happy in school. We were just taught what the powers that be want us to know. It didn't matter what we resonated with, regardless, we had to learn the things they taught. As an adult we can still continue to learn and grow and even question the things we were taught in school. We need to create our own Happiness School. We can learn about the things we actually want to learn, and learn how to find happiness in everything in our daily lives. We can also learn not to repeat the same mistakes we made earlier in our lives, and also learn what our higher purpose is. (More on that later.)

I see a school of happiness;
where love and consciousness grow.

Students learn to be happy,
and truly gifts will show.

In this school of love and light
they come to know the truth.

That we are here to serve each other
each senior, babe, and youth

Chapter Seven:

Creativity is Key

Everyone needs to have some sort of creative outlet. As was mentioned in the last chapter, we need to actively continue to outwardly express ourselves. Discovering and nurturing your passions adds depth and fulfillment to your journey. Writing music, poetry or short stories; painting, dancing and even making jewelry or woodworking are some creative examples. Self-expression is what makes us human. It is a way to let energy flow through our bodies. In dance or even in woodworking, for example, you are creating something and letting energy flow through your body to do it. It is a way to release any stored up emotions. Practice your connection to happiness every day with your own creativity.

Do you like music? Turn it on and dance like no one is watching at least once a day. Learn to play a musical instrument or learn a new song if you already play one. Make a playlist of the music that inspires you and do your challenging tasks to it. Keep your playlist of songs that inspire you with you so that you can play them when necessary and add to the list when you hear a new song that will fit your playlist. Music can heal the soul and calm your nerves. As mentioned in a previous chapter, there are songs that scientifically heal with certain frequencies and if you want to, you can also search for those tranquil songs and experiment with how you feel when you listen to them. If something doesn't make you feel good, stop listening to it. (The same thing is true with TV shows and films.)

Create a vision board for your happiness. You can be as creative as you let yourself. Get a large poster board and cut out photos from magazines, print out photos from the internet, or draw your goals and visions for things you discover that will make you happy. Put this in a prominent spot that you will see everyday to keep motivated. In your office, by your bed or nightstand, or by your bathroom mirror for example. Once you have accomplished something from your list, you can replace it with another idea or if you are happy with all of your goals and continue to be happy with them, just keep up the good happiness work! Let the vision board be a happy reminder of how far you have come on your journey!

Another great way to remind yourself of things that keep you happy and vibrant is to start a daily journal. Start off each entry with what you are thankful for or by recording the good vibe of the day. Of course, your thoughts aren't going to always be happy, but starting off and ending positive are key to bring about a peaceful and fulfilled life. The more you focus on the positive, (even in the darkest moments) the better you will feel and the better you will be able to cope with the darkness. Allow yourself to simply write out all of your thoughts and don't edit yourself. This isn't for others to see, but for you to allow yourself to see how you feel, acknowledge it, and move on. Make sure no matter what you feel, start and end each entry on a positive thought, even if it's just to say, "today will be better". You can write about your daily connection to happiness and call it "My happiness Journey". Life is, after all, a journey and some days will be merrier, and some will be more difficult than others. It's how you acknowledge and move on from the events that matter. Writing your feelings out can help you see them and make better choices for yourself.

Creative writing in general can be a very healing process. Do you like writing poems? Writing music? Maybe you would like to write a book? You can use your personal experiences and get them out onto paper. Not only will you create something that others may enjoy and learn from but you will also be getting your thoughts out of your head and onto the paper. This can be very cathartic. You don't ever have to show anyone. In fact, the first time you start writing you may want to say to yourself that this is something just for you. Maybe you will find your career or hobby from it as well. That can be said about any of the things you use to bring yourself happiness. They say the best films, music, etc are things written from the heart and not from someone trying to make something specific for the purpose of it's success.

Even if you have a very stressful job, not much spare time, or a job in a very technical field and think you have no time for something creative, I challenge you to find time to bring creativity into your life. Maybe you have always wanted to knit cat sweaters or make mosaic artwork. Whatever it can be, the important part of it is that you are taking time each day or perhaps 3 days a week (or the very least on the weekend) to give yourself a creative outlet. You will not only create things you feel proud of because you actually created them, but it will also give you an outlet to let off some steam and allow yourself a moment all to yourself.

If art or writing isn't something you think you can do (at least give it a try), perhaps give yourself permission to watch others create. Go to a play, a concert, or an art show. It may inspire you to try these things yourself, or it will at least show you the love others put into something. Love is contagious. Seeing other's fulfill their happiness can spark the desire for it in you.

Just remember that we are all different, so what makes one person happy doesn't necessarily make another person happy. Even if you think you don't have a creative bone in your body, I promise you that you do. It might not be singing, or writing, but maybe it's collecting rocks and making rock sculptures, or maybe it's organizing your kitchen cabinets in your own unique way. It doesn't matter what it is, just that you are allowing yourself some form of creative expression.

What are some of the creative things you might like to try? Painting? Ballroom dancing? Calligraphy? It could be ANYTHING that gets you out of your head and into a creative flow.

Here is some space to write a few of your own creative flow ideas.

1._____
_____
_____

2._____
_____
_____

3._____
_____
_____

Why is creativity so important to our happiness? I think it's because we can fully express ourselves in a way that is truly unique to us. Even if you are a painter and know other painters, none of you will create the same exact picture. It is your chance to create something that is your individual interpretation of reality.

How many times in our lives are we able to have free rein and create something with love and so much of ourselves included? The answer is as much as you allow yourself to. That is why it is so important to let your creative juices flow. It is your time. It is all yours. It is your creation.

Not only is it all yours, but it is your unique expression of how you see the world. It's a song you write from the feelings you feel. It's the dance you create with how you feel the music and the way you interpret the words. It's the painting you create from your view of someone or something. No one can take that from you because it is all yours. We don't have a choice on many things in life like paying bills (I mean we could choose not to but it wouldn't be advised) but we do have a choice on how we express ourselves creatively.

We are taught that miracles do not exist. Pretend that they do and see what happens. Think about the things you would like to manifest in your life. Write them down or create a vision board as mentioned before. I still recommend journaling. When you come up with things that you want, while you take your space every day to meditate and envision, know that they will happen. They are starting to happen for you right now. The more you create the space for yourself, the quicker you will see things manifest.

What are a few things you would like to manifest? Can you picture yourself doing these things? Can you picture your life when you achieve them? Write them here.

1._____

_____

2._____

_____

3._____

_____

Creativity is a gift
it's inside of us all.

No one is without it,
sometimes it just feels small.

Grow it and nurture it,
shower it with love.

Learn to express it,
as a gift from above.

Chapter Eight:

Happiness Isn't Alone

S o far, we have pretty much just used the word happy to define a pleasurable life. I mentioned that you could choose to be happy or choose to be sad. That is pretty much the crux of it, but obviously there are many words and feelings in between the two experiences. In this simple thought process, you have two choices. You can choose to be happy in spite of the crap that happens in your day or you can decide to allow the crap to take over and make you sad. You can also feel jovial, excited, grateful, loved, or any other positive emotion. In contrast, you could choose to feel depressed, bored, hateful, vengeful, or any other negative emotion.

I say you can choose because eventually, if practiced, you will see a choice between feeling a good or bad emotion. I am not saying you won't ever be sad or depressed or want revenge, but you will see that you are choosing to feel that way for longer than necessary if you start to practice acknowledging your emotions. If someone cuts you off on the freeway, for example, your first thought might be anger because they almost caused you to wreck your car, but will you choose to carry that emotion with you for the rest of the day? Or will you choose to acknowledge that maybe that person made a mistake and you allow the anger to happen but then release it and choose forgiveness and move on with your day? The person who chooses forgiveness and is grateful there wasn't a worse outcome will be able to experience a joyful experience a lot quicker than the one who holds onto that anger and goes home only to pick a fight with their loved one because they are still angry.

Yes, you need to acknowledge your feelings, but to hold onto negative thoughts longer than necessary will only cause you more grief in the long run. The sooner you can truly let go of anger, the sooner you can get back to feeling joy and love. It is always a choice. I know it's hard to accept that when someone or something has done you wrong, or you feel you were dealt a bad hand in life because of your circumstances. But the quicker you realize that you have the power in your choice, the better life you will lead. Yes, you might have to work harder or longer than someone else to achieve what you want but if you want to be truly happy you will. You will have a much easier journey with love than hate.

This is not to say you won't have bad days. We are human and to think we live in a rainbow and unicorn world would be ridiculous. It is how you choose to acknowledge and over come the bad days that will set you apart. If you journal and write each day, you can acknowledge that you are having a bad day and that you will try to have a better day tomorrow. Do something from your list of things that make you happy and try to set positive intentions.

Gratitude has a huge impact on happiness. One simple act of kindness can change everything. Gratitude has a transformative power to help shape a positive mindset. Besides writing in a journal, try writing thank you cards. They can be to yourself or to someone who has done something nice for you. A good practice is to come up with at least three things to be grateful for each day. Maybe write three thank you notes each day. Try it for a week and see how happiness follows you. It will also likely inspire others around you and make the day of the people you thank. Consider thanking that store clerk that went out of their way to help you, the doctor that took extra time to explain something to you, the mailman who made sure your mail wasn't wet from the rain. Think about how receiving a thank you note would make them feel. You will probably make someone's day brighter and in turn they will make someone else's day brighter and so on. Happiness and gratitude are contagious. Uncover the happiness found in acts of kindness and in contributing to the well being of others.

Who or what can you write thank you notes for right now?

1._____

2._____

3._____

Sometimes when you want to choose happiness, you will be bombarded with things that are trying to make you unhappy. Call it Murphy's Law, or call it a test, but it happens. You will want to call the whole thing off, but the challenging days that you get through will make you realize how much choosing happiness over anger is important for your soul. Some days there will be small steps ahead and large steps backwards but always have your intentions in mind.

Let's talk about the practicality of it all. There will be days when the weight of the world seems like it's just too heavy. We live in very trying times, and if you look around, sometimes it can be very overwhelming for those of us that have awakened to the reality of our world. So how do we rise above it? Because again, we only have one choice, happiness, or not happiness. At the end of the day, our time here is short, so what can we do to make it enjoyable?

One day at a time, set daily intentions, create your daily dose of happy. Here is an exercise for you to try. How many times have you felt love or joy today? You probably realize you feel it more than you think. Become aware of these moments throughout the day. These are great journal entries for your journal. Try and think of at least one instance in which you felt love or joy each day before bed. This is an incredibly beneficial practice. The more gratitude you have, the more gratitude you will experience. Remember, like vibrations and energy match like vibrations and energy.

Here are some things you can ask yourself and/or write down every day to start your morning out in the right direction. Instead of writing your answers here, start a journal where you can answer these questions daily.

1. What kind of moments or experiences do I want to have today?

2. How do I want to feel today?

3. What am I grateful for?

4. Today I will let go of _____. (Fill in the blank)

5. My future will be full of _____. (Fill in the blank)

6. Life is _____. (Fill in the blank)

7. When did I feel joy today?

Try this exercise for at least a week and examine how you feel. If it helped you, continue it. If it didn't, that's ok. Maybe try it again in a few weeks or months. You are the master of your reality and happiness. The more you choose happiness over fear, the better your quality of life will be.

Fear is what stops most people from achieving happiness or anything of quality in their life. When you realize the only real feeling is love, you will let go of fear. Fear is the absence of love. Fear puts us in fight or flight mode. It takes us out of our own human capabilities and takes us out of control of our own destiny. We are giving our power to someone or something else when we choose fear.

When combatting fear, ask yourself what are you afraid of and what is the worst thing that could happen. For example, if you are afraid to sing in front of a crowd because you might get judged, what is the worst that can happen? Maybe the worst that can happen is that you get judged by people that have their own opinions and own agenda. But the best thing that can happen is that you sing in front of the crowd, get a great response, and feel wonderful after conquering that fear. Maybe you find a new hobby or career. A fearful person will never know. Do something that scares you because if you accomplish it, it will make you greater than you ever thought you could be. If you aren't as successful as you would have liked, does it really matter? You at least tried and became better for it and you can keep trying until you are successful.

Obviously, someone who is being robbed has a much different experience with fear. When dealing with someone who is deliberately trying to hurt you, it carries with it a whole other set of circumstances. When we encounter this kind of fear it is still important to remain calm and in a vibration of love. I know it sounds crazy, but someone with a vibration of love will be handled and handles things better than someone who is in fear and fight or flight mode. The more you control your emotions and feelings, the better you can cope with anything that comes your way. We all know those people who we would turn to in an emergency because they are calm, cool, and collected about everything. Be one of those people by realizing you have control over anything that comes your way.

In the dance of life, we have many things to feel.
Twirling around is happiness versus fear.

Sometimes we're happy and sometimes we're sad.
As long as you let it, joy can be had.

Choose the path of light where love is found.
Fear gets diminished and radiance abounds.

Chapter Nine:

Relationships and Happiness

By loving and healing yourself, not only will you have an easier journey with emoting love, the people who become attracted to you as friends and intimate partners will be loving as well. Your energy is powerful and people attract like energies. A broken person will usually attract another broken person. Strengthen yourself and your relationships with loving, happy, forgiving energy. If you find yourself in a relationship that is not fulfilling, it might be time to reevaluate it and yourself. This is not to say the relationship should end, but perhaps a conversation about your feelings or the energy you are feeling from that relationship is necessary. Just remember that another person cannot make you happy. You are in control of that. If you find yourself consistently unhappy around a particular person, ask yourself what the root cause of that unhappiness might be. Did they lie to you? Did they do something to make you feel unloved? Or is it something inside of you instead, like jealousy? That is a conversation you need to have with them and/or yourself. Blaming them for you not being happy is giving someone else your power.

Are you always attracted to a particular type of person? The domineering woman or the bad boy type, for example. If you find yourself choosing the same negative traits in someone over and over again, it is time to see what you need to heal in your own life so that you can make healthier choices. Sometime we need to be shown our patterns and bad choices to start to make better choices that bring us closer to happiness. It is something that we will constantly be evaluating within ourselves our entire lifetime if we want to stay focused on bettering ourselves and bringing about our own well being and satisfaction. Then, we can be of better service to ourself and others.

When people say, "I had the happiness or pleasure of seeing you", it means you made them happy. That is a great feeling. It is what we long for. How many people do you actively do a good deed for or say something positive to each day? Are you thinking about how you can be of service to others? A fun exercise to try is to find a stranger each day and do or say something positive to them. Even telling someone something as simple as you love their smile can make that person's day. We are so caught up in what others are doing to us or inside our own heads that we forget about doing good things for others. It is amazing how much positive energy you will receive in return if you do a good deed each day.

You could also unknowingly carry your trauma and anger and fling it in other people's direction which is why it is important to always check yourself.

Getting in a car and driving after a heated argument might not be the best idea until you take the time to relax and let the anger go. Also, even more simply, a hurt person hurts others. This is not necessarily true physically but definitely mentally.

On the other hand, you could be someone that triggers another person not because of your anger but because of their jealousy or something within them that creates a negative feeling. This is never your fault (unless of course you are actively trying to get under their skin). It is that person's choice to feel a certain way just as it's your choice to feel a certain way. There won't be anything you can do to help that situation unless they become aware of their own traumas. Realize it is their issue and move on. Learn to disassociate yourself from these people's drama. Likewise, make sure you aren't inflicting your trauma onto others. Is there someone that makes you upset or you feel like they are sabotaging you? Whatever the negative feeling is, it's ok to end a relationship that is not creating positive energy. Just make sure to completely access the situation for what it is, otherwise the pattern will continue until you learn to heal or fix it.

Sometimes, like in the case of a family member or co-worker, you will simply have to learn to not take their energy on. If you must be around someone that throws off your happiness, learn to figure out why they upset you. Do they make you feel inferior? Do they say or do negative things around you?

Are they narcissistic? When you learn what the issue is, you can deflect it back to them because ultimately you are in charge of how you feel no matter the reasoning, and ultimately their actions are because of their issues not yours. You might also get a glimpse of who they truly are.

Many times when people bother us it is because of our own insecurities. If we are confident in ourselves, it is easier to deflect someone else's negativity. If you are already worried about your body image and someone calls you a slob, it will affect you more than someone who is confident. Also, if you think people aren't going to like you, guess what? They won't. The energy you are emitting will affect your reality.

Even if you are emitting positive energy, not taking on someone's energy is a strategy that needs to be learned. Some people are naturally good at it, but most of us need to work at it. Always be true to yourself and learn to smile and nod. Don't get caught up in their drama and learn to see when you do accidentally. It's hard to let people "win" with their digs and condescending attitudes, but once you learn to let these things go, watch their comments and attitudes change. If things don't bother you, they will stop.

Interestingly, most of the time when someone says or does rude things to you, it is a reflection on their own self doubt. Once you realize this, you can learn to take their derogatory attitude with a grain of salt. I know this isn't easy especially if you have to work or live with these people daily. I always find that the more mean and cranky people are, the more love they need. I know it sounds absurd and probably the last thing you want to give a jerk is more love, but watch what happens when you do.

This is not to say, make yourself crazy. If they are a jerk you can absolutely limit your interactions with them, but it's at least good for an experiment to see how they react to more love. They probably aren't used to getting it.

How many times have you had a party or invite only function and many of your invites didn't show up. These were the people who you thought to be your best friends or people you admired. It can be disheartening, but what about the people who did show up? They were there because they wanted to be. They didn't need to get something from it. They truly wanted to be there. (Many times people don't show up because they "found something better" to do.)

I joke that if I want to see who my true friends are, I need to invite them all to something and see who shows up. Certainly some legitimately can't make it, but it's the ones that are "maybes" that you need to question. Ultimately, it doesn't matter who shows up but that you are doing something that you love and those that are in your life for a purpose will show up.

Forget the ones that don't. If you have one true friend, that is more than many people have. Focus on what you have, not what you don't. Likewise, not being invited to something might upset you but think about if you really resonate with that person or persons anyway. It is usually a reflection of true purpose as to what you surround yourself with or what is surrounding you.

"Don't take it personally," is another mantra to take to heart. In the last example, people chose to not come to your function for whatever reason they had. Good, bad, or indifferent; that is their own agenda. They most likely don't have much love or true connections in their lives because they are always thinking of the superficial wins. What others can do for them is constantly on their mind. They need outside validation instead of looking into themselves. Send them love, know it was not a reflection of you, and move forward with your own purpose and love.

If you are looking outside yourself for connections, look inside yourself first. You can connect to others in a loving fashion when you can connect to yourself first. More on that later, but make sure you also love yourself.

Truly love yourself no matter your weight, your height, or your looks because it's not what's on the outside that matters, it's what's on the inside and how you connect to yourself. I know that is easier said than done and maybe you think it might be easier to love yourself if only you weighed 20 pounds less or if only you had blue eyes instead of brown, etc. I promise you, it's the package on the inside that has way more to love than what is on the outside. It's why the most attractive people still go out and get plastic surgery. They think they can be happier if only this or that changes on their body. I promise you, if you don't love yourself at this exact moment in time, changing anything on the outside won't change that.

If you want to be healthier, then yes! Lose 20 pounds, challenge yourself to exercise more, and eat healthier foods. Your health is important and I'm not saying you shouldn't try to better yourself. I am just saying that loving yourself shouldn't have stipulations. Be proud of yourself and champion your wins but don't love yourself only if you accomplish those things. Learn to love the body you have, and that one is you.

Self-love is the goal, but not self-absorbed. It is important to know the difference and realize it is important to be selfless. People who are self absorbed are that way because they either don't get enough love and are trying to demand it, because they don't really love themselves and feel like they have to prove it, or they value things over people. The more we realize our ego is in charge of our greed, the happier we can become. Remember, our purpose always answers the how can I serve question and it shouldn't be just about serving yourself. (More about that in chapter 11.)

What about the parent or family member that you haven't been able to have a healthy relationship with? It's true that you can pick your friends but your family is your family. Having a healthy relationship means you are able to communicate with them and not rely on their love to feel loved. You can live in a mutual space without pointing blame or guilt. There are some children that were blessed to have a healthy relationship where their parents and family members were truly nurturing. There are others that had narcissistic, self loathing, selfish ones.

Until you heal your trauma with these people, you will not be able to have a healthy relationship. Realize that these people probably have their own trauma that isn't healed and it is the reason for their actions. They may never come to terms with these things in their lifetime but you have the power to heal things for yourself. Once you realize you can't take these things others did to you personally, you can begin to forgive and heal. It isn't always fair and it isn't always easy, but it is your choice. Do you want to be happy or not? Stop putting the happiness card on someone else. Saying, "they did this to me," or, "they treated me horribly," won't help you heal. Forgiveness and the realization that what they did was their journey needs to be realized and that needs to be forgiven and healed by you.

This doesn't mean you have to choose to have a daily relationship with these people. All you have to do is forgive them and yourself. What kind of relationship you choose to continue to have will depend on your healing and their healing. Some people are not capable of love because they don't give it to themselves. They need to heal themselves and just like they can't heal you, you can't heal them. It's sad to realize that some of the people you love aren't helping themselves, but remember that even though your journey's came together for a purpose at one point, it doesn't mean they are on the same path as you. You are not in control of anyone's destiny or happiness except your own. This is your journey to happiness. Everything is always your choice.

What are a few of your favorite relationships, after yourself of course?

1._____

2._____

3_____

What are the relationships that need fixing or re-evaluating?

1._____

2._____

3._____

What can you learn about yourself from the relationships you have? For example, are you listening to your inner voice? Are you holding on to relationships that no longer serve you? Are you in healthy relationships with those that want the best for you? Are you learning to love yourself before taking on other's baggage and are your relationships contributing to your growth?

1._____
_____
_____

2._____
_____
_____

3._____
_____
_____

It is important to remember that meaningful connections in our lives are what we should be building. Maintaining these are what contribute to our well-being and happiness. Anyone that doesn't contribute to your ultimate well being probably is on a different path than you. People will come and go from your life, and that is just a fact of life. Sometimes it is hard to let people go, but it is necessary for both of you for your souls to grow, learn, and lead a purpose filled life. Happiness lies in unity, and sometimes it allows us to see the differences in people and the different paths we must take.

Relationships can be fulfilling,

or they can be hard to bear.

It's important to love yourself firstly,

then great friendships will always be there.

Chapter Ten:

Success and Happiness

What is success? You can have all the money in the world and be what others perceive as successful and yet still be very unhappy. I believe that in order to be truly successful, you must achieve happiness. It must be your own happiness and not someone else's. A big house like your neighbor's or wealth like your uncle's won't fulfill you if you aren't being true to yourself and are just trying to be a copy of someone else.

Many people who are deemed rich or successful in their field of employment are not happy. Sometimes this is because they have to work harder to keep their status and wealth or they possibly purchased more so they are still paying off debt. It's also perhaps because they have given up part of themselves to devote to becoming successful in their field and now they are numb to other things. Money has nothing to do with how happy you are. You may think having a lot of money will make you happier but without the proper mindset and choices, you still won't be happy as a millionaire.

Have you heard of the term minimalist? Someone leading a minimalist lifestyle chooses to live with fewer possessions as opposed to needing lots of superficial things in their lives, like expensive cars and extra large houses. Most people who become minimalists have discovered that working longer hours and sacrificing time with loved ones and not doing things they love, are not worth it just to be able to buy things they don't really need to achieve happiness. People are made to be loved and things are made to be used. Unfortunately, some people get that backwards because of their love of things. Unhappy people use people and love things. Sounds backwards doesn't it? Loving things won't get you much love in return. You can't go to bed and snuggle with a fancy car and you can't feel joy just by having a bigger house. You will still face the same problems and struggles with your happiness.

You can be successful, have a lot of money, and be happy. I wouldn't say that you can't, but it is not a guarantee. A winning formula would include allowing yourself time to do the things you love with people that you love. So if you find yourself putting too much time into work just to buy things, it might be time to rethink your strategy. The grass is always greener. It always looks better on the other side of the fence, but it rarely is. Rich people still have problems. Poor people think that if they only had money they could be happier. Wherever you stand in the money department, there is always something more you can want. It's when you become happy with what you have and look to new experiences that you will find happiness. You have to be happy before you have the money.

Making a living is not the same thing as making a life. Making time for things you love along with making an income is more than important, it's essential to one's happiness. We all know someone who is a workaholic. Maybe it's you. Do you work long hours and say no to outings with friends and family just to keep up with your job? I'm sure there are people who think their job makes them happy. In fact, I do believe you must love your job. My philosophy is, do what you love and the money will come. Definitely love what you do because life is too short to spend time at something you are miserable doing. Even if you love your job, spending too much time at it and ignoring friends and family could be a sign that you are avoiding something else in your life.

Many of us are working just to make an income or because we don't have a choice if we are supporting a family, but this is why it is very important to make time to really live. Enjoy the little things. If you hate your job, make the best of it. Walk part of the way to work to take in nature before you clock in that day or spend your lunch hour writing poems. Take every opportunity to make the best of what you have to work with. Maybe your hobby, your creative outlet, is something you can turn into a job one day. It's hard to take the leap when others are counting on us to pay bills, but you can still make time to do the things that make you happy. Don't get stuck making a living without remembering to live.

It's also easy to get stuck on the thought of bringing in a lot of income just to be able to buy lots of things we think we need, or our family thinks they need. This goes back to the happiness school. What can we teach ourselves and our family about the things we think we need? Make a list of things you think you need on a monthly or yearly basis. Have your kids, if they are old enough, make a list of things they think they need. Now ask yourself and them if those things are more important than time spent with each other. Would they rather have the thing or be able to play ball in the backyard with you? Would you rather have the thing or spend the time with them creating a fort or watching a movie together? Time goes by fast. Before you know it, the time you could spend with each other is gone. Memories and the way you teach yourself and your kids to live will be more important to the future than any thing you could buy will be. That pair of shoes or outfit will be outdated or outgrown and forgotten but memories live forever.

What are the things that you think you need? Sometimes we might really need them. Sometimes we don't. It's up to you to decide.

1._____

2._____

Sometimes we get stuck on not only wanting specific things to be happy, but we also put so much emphasis on an upcoming event or even the thought of only being happy when it happens, that we lose site of the joy during the path to get there. Maybe you think you will feel successful only when you achieve a certain something or you think life will be better when you reach a certain goal. The problem with this is that these things rarely meet our expectations and when you put all of your hopes on a future event or thing, you miss out on the gift of now – the present. Living in the present will help you learn to see life's daily happiness.

Think about the couple preparing for their wedding. They put so many exceptions on that day that sometimes the planning becomes a stressful job and the couple believes that all their joy will only come through on the day of the wedding. The real joy in planning a wedding is the planning of it. Enjoy tasting the cake, enjoy making an invite list, and enjoy planning everything with your partner and know that the planning needs to be just as enjoyable as the event. The event will happen in a blink of an eye, but the time leading up to it and the time after it are what will be remembered.

What are some of the events or plans in your life that you put more stress on the day than the joy of planning it? Some things could be a party, retirement, or a big vacation.

Success is being able to be happy and enjoy each day no matter what. When you know you are doing your best and you live in each beautiful moment, you might even find happy surprises along the way. For example, it shouldn't matter that you didn't get that promotion. On the bright side, you may have more time with your family or there may even be a better fit job or promotion waiting for you around the next corner.

What if your car breaks down? You are probably angry about it, but while waiting for a tow truck you have time to look at the area you are in and discover the cutest coffee shop. You would never have seen it otherwise, so even the dismalest parts of our day can be a blessing in disguise. Look for these moments, because it is in these situations that make us stop and look around us that we will find unexpected joy.

Success is defined differently by everyone. Most people discover that money or things won't make them feel any better than those who own nothing. It's what we have besides these things and what lives inside us that matter.

What are the things that define success for you?

1._____
_____
_____

2._____
_____
_____

3._____
_____
_____

Success can be hard for the greedy.

They want to get rich overnight.

It's the ones that find love in each moment,

that will flourish and make their life bright.

Chapter Eleven:

Love, Connection, and Purpose

When it's dark enough, you can see the stars. Sometimes, we go through dark times to get to experience the light. One of the main things that can make us feel unhappy is forgetting who we truly are, lack of connection, or not knowing what our purpose is. We all long for love, connection, and purpose.

Often our purpose connects to how we can serve others. Thinking of how we can serve others takes the focus off of oneself and the ego. This allows us to connect to the world around us without getting caught up in jealousy or trying to be something we aren't.

Some people are just born knowing what they want to do with their life. They know they want to be a doctor and heal people or be a football player because they have an exceptional gift for that sport. Others struggle with what our purpose is. We don't know who we are supposed to be and let it weigh us down with the grief of not knowing.

Sometimes we have our purpose, but something happens along the way, like an injury or life experience that prohibits us from continuing with that same dream or purpose. This also sends grief into our life. It can be even more challenging because now we have anger associated with our original purpose.

But what if these things are to bring you to your real purpose? What if your real purpose wasn't to play football but to coach it, or even deeper, help people overcome the trauma that you faced while going through the process of getting a new purpose or goal.

Our real purpose here on earth is to be of service to others. It is how we overcome the darkness and move into the light. It is how we become true to ourselves and the universe. You may be an exceptional athlete, but it's what you do off the court or field that helps you define your purpose. Are you a good person, not just a good athlete? Do you want to see the good in everyone? Or are you around just to see what people have to give you?

How do you connect to others? Sometimes how we connect to others defines our purpose. Like minded people will find each other if they are open to it. For example, if you like to take yoga classes you will probably find others that like yoga if you go to yoga classes. It sounds silly to say that because it's so obvious but many times we don't do things when we are alone. We forget there are others out there who enjoy doing the same things we do. You will find like minded people doing like minded things. Maybe when you meet these new people in yoga classes they will introduce you to other things that you will grow to love. You just have to be willing to connect to new people and things.

Maybe not only will you connect to people and things through others, but you will also help connect others to people and things you love as well. Maybe your purpose was to connect two people together or perhaps they were supposed to connect you to someone or something. The world is vast but it is still small.

When we talk about connection, most forget the most important connection is to oneself. Sometimes it can be painful to connect to oneself. If there is still trauma that hasn't been resolved, it might be more difficult. The connection to oneself is the most important one because when you truly connect and listen to yourself, you will have the most peace, love, and purpose in your life. You won't need other people or things to make you happy. Take time to really listen to yourself. Is there a voice that tells you to hurry up, or that you're not good enough? This means you have some unresolved trauma somewhere. We are not perfect so naturally we will make mistakes but no one should constantly beat themselves up.

It is when one isn't able to connect to oneself that they try to connect to other causes, people, and things. This is not always bad because we are here to serve others so if you see a fellow human in need, absolutely help if you can. It is when the reasons get muddled that you need to be careful. This is why people join cults or organizations that promise connections and success, etc. They aren't comfortable with themselves and reach outward to feel love and connection. Trust me when I say these cults and organizations either know this or they have such big egos that they need you to make them feel loved back. Most of the time, it's both.

Cult leaders and members need this connection to feel safe, loved, connected, and to have a purpose. It is easy for people outside to see the dangers but not easy for those involved because they feel all those things. If you can't feel a connection to yourself, you will get lost in other's agendas. This will not create long term happiness. This is not your purpose but someone else's.

How do you know if you are subscribing to purpose, connection, and love outside of yourself? For one, you will not be comfortable with your own thoughts. You will take others words and ideas as your own. Does something feel right, or does it feel instinctually wrong? Always do your own research. Don't take someone else's propaganda as a truth unless you have done your own research on it.

One truly cannot connect to others in a positive way without being able to connect with oneself. Once you connect to yourself, it will be easy to see and do the things that make you happy and serve your purpose.

So how do you connect to yourself? Meditation, journaling, healing your traumas, etc. It is a lifelong work in progress. Traumas sound so horrible but they could be something as simple as you were told by your teacher you weren't smart enough once, or you were the last person picked for a game of kickball on your street. We take these experiences and store them in the back of our minds. We behave badly to others because of them and don't usually know why. It is only when we truly listen to ourselves and what we are telling ourselves that we can heal.

Sometimes traumas can be complicated like ancestral ones. These are feelings and thought processes that cloud our judgements because they have been ingrained or taught since birth or before. It takes a lot of self taught education to get rid of old beliefs. Just like the cult mind, many of these were taught to us because of someone else's agenda. It is going back to that happiness school in earlier chapters. We can never be done teaching ourselves our own truths. No one else is going to come along and save you. You need to save yourself.

If something someone says or does affects you to the point of anger or unhappiness, you need to check in with your ego. You also most likely have some sort of issues or trauma you need to work through. Remember, it is always your choice to be happy and always your choice to not be. Clear out the anger and what caused it and you can be happy.

So, if we find ourselves subscribing to other people's purposes and not our own, how do we know what our purpose is? I think a good way to start is by asking yourself, how can I be of service to others? Maybe you are good at connecting people and want to become a head hunter or maybe you feel like you are on a healing journey and want to share what you have learned with others. It can be as educational or as spiritual as feels right for you.

Sometimes your job is different than your purpose, especially in the infancy stages when you first discover your purpose. If, for example, you want to be a musician and share your music with others but can't make a living yet doing that, you will have to find a job that you can pay your bills with while pursuing music. Maybe you can work in a similar field like a receptionist at a record label or teach music to kids while you gain fans. Just make sure it is something that can still help you on your happiness journey.

Maybe you love your job as an accountant and it more than pays your bills but you still want to express yourself more creatively or have a deeper purpose. What else can you do to be in service and connect to others? Maybe you also love animals so you decide to volunteer at a local animal shelter. Maybe you decide you want to teach at-risk kids cooking or art classes after work each day.

To be in service to others doesn't mean you need to look outside of your family and friends either. Are you a parent with small kids? Do you have an older parent or disabled sibling that need a helping hand? It is important to realize that your kids, spouse, or maybe even extended family could also use your expertise with anything that you might have to offer. Sometimes we don't have to look further than our own backyard for the opportunity to serve and connect to others.

Our service to others and even our connections will probably change throughout our lives depending on where we are at in our life's journey. Someone who just graduated from high school is going to have a much different lifestyle than someone who is retired and looks after their grandkids each day. Just always listen and be in connection with yourself and you will know what you need for happiness.

Think about your purpose. Many times it connects with your given gifts and talents. Putting your gifts out into the world will connect you to a purpose filled life. This connection will bring about happiness and love through connection and unity.

Think of 3 things that are uniquely your gifts.
YES! You have gifts. Meditate or journal about them
if you are struggling with what they are. Stop being
hard on yourself because you wouldn't be here if you
weren't a unique blessing with many gifts to offer.
(Maybe you are a good communicator or
compassionate listener, an animal whisperer, a
polished musician, or a creative parent.)

1._____
_____

2._____
_____

3._____
_____

Now think about things you love to do, or things/
people you love to be around. (Again, this could be
music, animals, children, nature, etc.) What are they?

1._____
_____

2._____
_____

3._____
_____

Knowing your gifts and the environment you love to be in can help you find your purpose. For example, if you find that you are empathic towards animals and love being around them, you might find happiness working in a veterinarians office, an animal shelter, or perhaps you want to become a spokesperson for animal rights. This could be a hobby or a job for you. This new discovery may bring about a job change or it may be something you volunteer at until a job opens up or you discover you purpose elsewhere.

What are a few ideas of a purpose that could fulfill you?

1._____

_____

_____

2._____

_____

_____

3._____

_____

_____

Sometimes it's hard to connect our gifts and connections with a purpose. Sometimes the timing has to be right and you may have to put in place a sort of temporary purpose until you find your main one. Your purpose may also shift as you grow.

You might start off making music in the pop scene because you want to inspire others with your words, but then discover it didn't fulfill you because your voice wasn't heard so you start teaching music to youth and become another's inspiration. Sometimes one purpose can lead to another. Just remember to love each new discovery about yourself and the world and remember to enjoy the process. The process should be as gratifying as the place you end up. This is all a part of your journey here on earth and as long as you are connected to your true self, you can continue to be connected to purpose, love, and happiness.

Happiness finds connections,

to ourselves and those we love.

To be true to our purpose we strive for,

it connects us below and above.

When we listen to what our heart tells us,

happiness flows every day.

Even in dark times or hardships,

we know we will be ok.

Chapter Twelve:

The Journey is for Life

There will always be points in our lives when change comes about and we must reevaluate and reshape our happiness. Regard each new life event as if you were birthing a baby. New events are like births and must be given the proper time and energy. Think about your life time and events that will shape you.

Birth, preschool, adolescence, college, parenthood, middle age, empty nesters, senior living, and the many in between; these are a few of the many stages we can go through in life. Each stage will bring about different goals, issues, and paths to happiness. The person you were as a child is not the same person you will be as an empty nester. Yes, the core of you is still there, but hopefully you will have grown and learned new things along the way. Sometimes new issues will shape you and hopefully you don't hold on to too much trauma or other people's drama. The people you choose to surround yourself with, the things you watch and read, as well as the conversations you participate in will shape your life and who you become.

Every stage in life has it's own choices, lessons, and beauty. Sometimes we have to relearn how to be happy in a new set of parameters but ultimately it is still our choice. Each day we are given new wonderful life lessons to add to our library of self. Sometimes we have to be a parent to ourself. Ask yourself what you can learn from a particular situation or person, even if the experience wasn't the best.

When you are a child and need to adhere to parental and school rules, it is a lot different than when you are the parent or teacher making the rules. You may however slip into your past self and end up feeding those same draconian methods that were taught to you back to the children you teach. If you don't over come the trauma you faced as a child, you will unleash your trauma onto others. If you don't understand who you truly are, you can't expect to teach others.

We are so worried about what a child needs to learn from us that we forget that we are going to learn from the child. We can learn about our own insecurities or our own traumas because they're going to be brought up as the child grows. It's like a mirror into our soul if you let it be. It should be an open communication while yes, we need to teach the child life skills and what not, there's so much that we can learn from children if we listen to them. Make it more of a conversation instead of a student and teacher mentality.

Even as a parent, we can learn from our children. We are now in a society where we are starting to see that we can learn from each other. What lessons are your children teaching you? Perhaps they are teaching you patience or how to love unconditionally. What lessons are you teaching them? Ultimately, we learn and love every single day if we are open and acknowledge it. It is a beautiful relationship when everyone understands how we can learn from each other and balance our lives with love.

Speaking of balancing our lives, what is your relationship to life and love? Are you open to receiving love and a love filled life? Try not to get seduced by things that take you away from being open to that and who you really are. These are the lessons you can teach to the children in your life and the people you surround yourself with as well as yourself. By living this sort of life, you will ultimately inspire those around you as well as yourself. You teach by example without even knowing it.

All of our stages in life bring about learning and new paths to happiness. Senior citizens can learn from toddlers, just as toddlers can learn from senior citizens. Everyone and everything in our lives teach us the path to life and happiness and love. We are in a constant state of growth or stagnation. We can grow from things or become complacent to whatever the universe picks for us.

No one is going to save us. We must save ourselves. We must take responsibility for how we act and feel. If you are going to walk away from this book with any one concept, my hope is that you take to heart the fact that you are in control of choosing happiness. It may not always feel like it, but it is a simple principle. Everything in life is a choice.

You can make excuses for things that you choose, but ultimately you are the one that chooses. I doubt that someone will ever hold you down and demand you to be happy or unhappy. Even if they did, it is still a choice.

Our choices shape our lives and our happiness. This is what karma is. Karma does exist but so does free will. You have the power and ability to change things in your life and your karma.

Surround yourself with happy people whenever you have the choice to do so. Happy energy is contagious. But so is negative energy so remember that. When it comes to connection, you're going to connect to the people that you are vibrating with so if you have trauma, you will connect to people with trauma similar to yours. However, if you must be around unhappy people for whatever reason, remember their journey is not yours unless you choose to let their energy into your world.

The most crucial aspect of being happy often involves cultivating a positive mindset and embracing gratitude. Finding contentment in the present moment, appreciating what you have, and fostering positive relationships are fundamental to lasting happiness. Just remember this life is yours, so everything you decide is ultimately your choice. Be authentic and don't try to be someone else. Love yourself in every good and bad moment, and choose happiness. Let this be your roadmap to a life of joy and fulfillment. My hope is that you continue to pursue the school of happiness.

On winding roads we step with grace.

Some dance, some skip, others tread untraced.

Through valleys low and peaks so tall.

Our journey to happiness will forever call.

One request.

We'd love to hear from you.

How is your happiness journey going? What inspired you from the book? Check out our website www.anchorheartbooks.com and let us know. Paula personally reads all of your comments and reviews. If you have a moment please leave a review of this book too (link on website). Let's create a huge Quest for Happiness community and spread love and joy.

www.ingramcontent.com/pod-product-compliance
Lightning Source LLC
Chambersburg PA
CBHW070724130626
46553CB00005B/2142